Original title:
Waves Upon the Shore

Copyright © 2025 Creative Arts Management OÜ
All rights reserved.

Author: Beckett Sinclair
ISBN HARDBACK: 978-1-80581-680-5
ISBN PAPERBACK: 978-1-80581-207-4
ISBN EBOOK: 978-1-80581-680-5

Reflections on the Water

Floating like a duck on the stream,
I ponder life like it's all a dream.
Then a fish jumps up, starts to laugh,
And I spill my drink—it's just my half.

Sunshine dances like it knows a joke,
The gulls are squawking, oh what a hoax!
I wave back at clouds, they wave in return,
As I balance my hat on a log that won't burn.

Sirens of the Salt Marsh

The crabs are clapping, what a wild show,
While the seagulls croon songs, you know how they go.
A clam tries to dance, but it slips on a shell,
And my picnic sandwich just fell in as well.

Frogs in their chorus, quite the charade,
They serenade marshes with all of their spade.
A heron rolls eyes as it watches the scene,
While I try not to trip over roots that are mean.

Journeying Between Tides

Sandcastles rise, oh what a delight,
But then comes a wave—they're gone out of sight!
Children are laughing, chasing the foam,
While I search for my flip-flop, forgot it at home.

Seashells and treasures appear from the deep,
A crab scurries by, in a hurry to leap.
Uncle Joe's sunburn is the talk of the day,
As he turns the same color as ketchup, hooray!

Elysium at Sea Level

Sunsets are painted with burgers and fries,
The seagulls are eyeing my picnic surprise.
They swoop and they dive, it's a feathered ballet,
While I guard my chips, and keep the crumbs at bay.

With each generation, we build our great forts,
Only to find them washed out by reports.
But laughter's the currency shared on this scene,
Till we all end the day with a splash and a scream.

Beneath the Celestial Waves

The fish wear hats, it's quite a sight,
They gossip loudly, day and night.
A crab in shades, so cool, so bold,
Telling tales of treasures untold.

A dolphin dances, a clumsy leap,
As seagulls squawk, and do not sleep.
The starfish laughs, with eight arms wide,
While octopus plans its stylish ride.

Calligraphy of the Current

A mermaid writing, oh what a task,
With scales that shimmer and questions to ask.
She jots down jokes on a shell so neat,
While shrimp hold a party, patting their feet.

With bubbles of laughter that fill the air,
They share silly puns without a care.
The seaweed giggles in playful green,
As a clam hides secrets, a quiet queen.

Chasing the Horizon's Breath

The sun chases shadows with a golden grin,
While crabs in limos cruise off with a spin.
The tide plays tricks, like hide and seek,
As crabs throw a dance, it's all quite unique.

With surfboards shaped like bananas and pears,
The fish become surfers, without any cares.
They laugh and they splash, a watery chase,
Under the skies, it's a silly race.

Portraits of the Shore

Each shell a canvas, each grain a dream,
Seagulls pose proudly, or so it would seem.
A beach ball bounces on sand so fine,
As jellyfish waltz, a rhythmic divine.

The sandcastle wizards craft towers of might,
While kids build moats, oh what a sight!
The goofy sea cucumber strikes a pose,
And giggles erupt from the starfish rows.

The Tempest's Heartbeat

A seagull stole my sandwich,
With a caw and a swoop so bold.
I chased it down the sandy path,
While my friends just laughed and rolled.

The clouds above were rumbling,
Like a hungry belly's growl.
Nature's big joke on me,
As I ran like some mad fowl.

The tide came in quite quickly,
Dancing around my feet.
I lost my flip-flop in the splash,
Now I'm left with mismatched feet.

But laughter filled the air,
With each bumbling stumble.
In this wild, salty playground,
It was impossible not to tumble.

Where Seafoam Dreams

The sea looked quite inviting,
With foam like whipped cream on pie.
I dove in for a cool reprieve,
But swallowed salt instead—oh my!

A crab gave me a sideways glance,
As if I were the strangest sight.
I danced like I was on hot coals,
While avoiding his claws with delight.

Seagulls squawked a loud review,
Critiquing my lack of grace.
I waved back like an overgrown kid,
Who can't quite keep a straight face.

The tide pulled back with a chuckle,
As I emerged, seaweed crowned.
In this ocean of giggles,
I found joy, my heart unbound.

Tales from the Briny Abyss

Fish gossip in schools, they say,
With tales of adventures grand.
One claimed it surfed a jellyfish,
And I nearly dropped my sandwich hand.

A clam with a fancy shell,
Reported a mermaid's song.
But every time I got close,
The clam just said, "Oh, you're wrong!"

A dolphin zipped by with flair,
Claiming to beat the tide.
I laughed at the ocean's banter,
As he took another ride.

In this watery comedy,
Laughter is never scarce.
With treasures of mirth and folly,
Life's a splash without a care.

Shadows on the Beach

Footprints tracked in soft, warm sand,
Whose are these? Not mine, I swear!
I followed them a little ways,
But ended up in a seagull's snare.

The sun played peek-a-boo with clouds,
Like kids in a game of hide.
I lost my hat to a strong wind,
And swore the ocean was on my side!

My shadow danced on the shore,
Doing moves I'd never try.
I mimicked it with a silly jig,
And folks nearby just wondered why.

As laughter rang like bells in air,
The beach became a stage.
Embraced by sun, sand, and giggles,
I left worries at the page.

Driftwood Dialogues

A stick named Gary took a stroll,
To find a hat that would be whole.
He met a crab, who said with glee,
"Why not try my hat? It's free!"

Gary laughed, his plan in hand,
He'd strut around just like a band.
But crabs don't wear hats, said the sea,
"Just grab some kelp, and dance with me!"

Lighthouses in the Mist

On a foggy night, it stood so tall,
A beacon bright, it had a ball.
"Is there anyone there?" it called out loud,
A clam replied, "Just a lonely crowd!"

"How odd! I thought I'd find some friends,
Not shells and sand, where the fun ends!"
Then it laughed so hard, it shook its head,
"Guess I'll just light up my own bed!"

Celestial Reflections

Stars twinkled down in a playful mood,
While sea turtles danced to a catchy tune.
"When life gives you waves, just float in style,
Don't just drift, give the ocean a smile!"

A fish in a tux, with jellyfish ties,
Said, "Join our bash, there's cake in the skies!"
And as glimmers sparkled on ocean's floor,
They raised a toast: "Let's shine evermore!"

Tidal Dreams

A dreamer once wished for a beachy throne,
With sandcastle walls, he'd never roam.
But waves giggled high at his grand parade,
"Your crown of shells will surely fade!"

Yet he built with fervor, ignoring the tide,
"I'll stay dry!" he exclaimed, with pride.
But blushing waves crashed with cheeky delight,
Turning his throne into a waterslide!

Moonlit Schemes

Beneath the bright, giggling moon,
Crabs plotted fun, a merry tune.
"Let's host a race on the sandy trail!"
The shells all clapped, like a flashy sale!

But slippery trails made them slide and glide,
With twists and turns they could hardly hide.
And laughing loud through the evening glow,
They danced on the sand—what a slapstick show!

Serenade of the Sea

Saltwater taffy goes astray,
Seagulls steal my lunch today.
My sandwich floats in ocean's breeze,
While crabs dance slow, with silly tease.

Starfish practicing ballet moves,
Jellyfish groove with loopy grooves.
The ocean sings in giggly tones,
As I chase fish with funny bones.

Dance of the Surf

Flip-flops flop with every stride,
As puddles laugh and run to hide.
A belly flop, the crowd will cheer,
While clams wear hats, it's quite a year!

Turtles twirl in beachside cheer,
While I trip over my last beer.
The rhythm of the salty spree,
Makes every laugh a jubilee.

Secrets Beneath the Foam

Seashells whisper wildest dreams,
While octopuses plot funny schemes.
Crabs in tuxedos on the prowl,
With seaweed ties, they strut and growl.

Mermaids giggle at sunburned fools,
Playing games in their watery pools.
A dolphin winks, it's quite a show,
As I get drenched from head to toe!

Horizon's Embrace

Kites are tangled in seaweed trees,
As fishermen bicker with bumblebees.
The breeze tickles my sandy nose,
While a crab criticizes my pose.

Laughter echoes with ocean's clap,
As I take a tumble, fall on a map.
With sun hats flying, the fun won't cease,
In this comedy of waves, I find my peace.

Sands of Time

As grains of sand take flight,
They giggle in the sunlight.
Tossing shoes, we start to race,
Against the tide, our stairs misplaced.

A crab watched us with one eye,
Making waves as we sprinted by.
Our picnic's now a dinner dance,
With seagulls plotting their advance.

The clock tick-tocks like a seal,
Wiggling dreams we can't conceal.
Each hourglass slip, a silly cheer,
Tomorrow's beachball is finally here!

Sea of Stories

The tide brings tales both old and new,
Like fishy gossip in a shoe.
We laugh at mermaids stuck in nets,
While pirates trade for seaweed pets.

Conch shells echo ancient pranks,
As dolphins flock to join our ranks.
Flip-flops clapping like applause,
While shells hide secrets, without a cause.

A lighthouse blinked its bright blue eye,
As crabs debated the ocean's pie.
With sandy toes and joyful shouts,
We sketch our stories in sea and doubts.

Call of the Nautical Horizon

The horizon beckons with a wink,
While sailboats race, and dolphins think.
Tugging on our joy, like a kite,
We chase the sun, it's quite a sight!

Seagulls squawk their daily gossip,
While waves laugh like a sloshing mop.
We wonder where the tide will send,
Our silly hopes, like fish, to bend.

The horizon giggles with a gleam,
As we sail forth, chasing a dream.
Life's a splash in this painted blue,
With every turn, a fresh debut!

The Cradle of the Ocean

In the cradle of water's jest,
We float on laughs, an endless quest.
A jellyfish floats with a grin,
As we splash around, let the fun begin!

Fish dance like they've won a prize,
Their scales glinting under sunlit skies.
We tumble in surf, then back to breathe,
While seaweed glows like funny wreaths.

The ocean's lullabies play on repeat,
With rhythms tickled by sandy feet.
Crabs join in with a tap-tap cheer,
As laughter and splashes fill the sphere.

Chronicles Through the Tide

Grab a shell, let's spin a tale,
Of kraken jokes and adventurous gale.
The tide rolls in with a cheeky shout,
Whispering secrets we can't live without.

A clam joins in, "I'll take a stab,"
While starfish roll, preparing the lab.
We scribble our stories in soft sea foam,
Creating mishaps in our sandy home.

Laughter spills like pebbles tossed,
While waiting for the mermaid who lost.
Chronicles weave through adventure's stream,
In this funny ocean where we all dream.

The Nautilus' Soliloquy

Oh, floating shell with spiral flair,
You boast of grace, yet hide in lair.
Your neighbors swim with such delight,
While you just sigh, what a boring plight!

With silly thoughts of treasure troves,
You dream of gold where nobody roves.
And all the fish laugh as they flee,
From your grand hopes of a perfect spree.

Your house is cozy but a bit aloof,
You talk to crabs, it's the ultimate goof.
Bubbles burst with every snicker,
As ocean life just gets slicker!

So, nautilus, wear that proud smirk,
In the sea's grand joke, you are the perk.
While others jump, splash, run, and dive,
At least you know you're still alive!

Songs of the Salty Breeze

The breeze it teases, oh what a brat,
It tickles your nose and fluffs your hat.
With whispers sweet as a sailor's song,
It swirls the sand, where does it belong?

It carries tales from beneath the tide,
Of pirates lost and mermaids who bide.
"Hey look!" shouts a gull, "I found a shoe!"
The salty breeze just says, "Oh, boo-hoo!"

With a giggle it tugs at your sleeve,
A gentle prank, you scarcely believe.
It shrieks with laughter and pulls at your hair,
Throwing confetti of seafoam everywhere!

So dance and prance with the playful air,
For in its chaos, there's joy to share.
Join the nonsense, let worries cease,
With songs of laughter, we'll find our peace!

An Elegy for the Distant Horizon

Oh horizon, you tease, so far yet near,
You promise adventures with nothing to fear.
But I'm stuck here counting grains of sand,
While you beckon me to your distant land.

A ship in the distance, it sways side to side,
But I'm tied to my blanket like a stubborn tide.
The ocean may call with a siren's charm,
But I've got snacks here, they keep me warm!

Your sunsets might glow in splendid hues,
But I trade in dusk for my comfy shoes.
So sail on, dear friend, explore the unknown,
I'll just wave from my recliner, alone.

Yet, one day perhaps, a whim will grip me,
To leave my recline and the safety of tea.
But for now, dear horizon, stay out of my sight,
While I munch popcorn and rest for the night!

The Seafarer's Solace

Oh, captain of chaos upon the blue,
With compass spinning, what's a sailor to do?
His maps are drawings from last week's lunch,
Navigating dishes, not waves, just a hunch!

The sextant's lost, but the snacks are near,
He settles for biscuits and a gin and beer.
With clouds as his friends, he sings out loud,
"Let's conquer the sea!" to a seagull crowd.

Swabbing the deck with his trusty mop,
He dreams of gold and a soda pop.
"Yo ho!" he laughs as he slips on the deck,
And it seems even Poseidon shakes his neck!

So relish the antics on this big ol' boat,
Where laughter is currency, in every note.
For the journey is wild, and the sea's full of glee,
It's the seafarer's solace, forever carefree!

A Symphony of Salty Air

The seagull squawks a merry tune,
As crabs dance beneath the moon.
I try to sing along with zest,
But sand gets stuck—I must confess.

The beach ball flies, it makes a trip,
And bounces off a sunburned hip.
My friend leaps up, but with a frown,
He tumbles over, graceless clown.

A toddler giggles, splashes about,
While wet dogs shake, causing a shout.
A flip-flop flings, it's airborne now,
A fashion statement? Not quite how!

The sun sets low, a golden glow,
Yet someone's stuck in a sandcastle dough.
We laugh so hard, we lose our breath,
In salty air, we jest with death.

Serenity in Shifting Sands

A sand dune whispers, quiet as night,
But my picnic ants are ready to bite.
I tried to lay back, enjoy the breeze,
Yet seagulls swoop down, aiming to tease.

The cooler spills, soda's a blast,
We're laughing so hard, I've spilled my glass.
With jelly sandwiches made for two,
They've joined the sand—wish they could chew!

Sunburned noses and hats askew,
Shifting sands bring sandy stew.
We dig and we dig, till someone yells,
"Found a starfish! Or is that a shell?"

Serenity sings, but we can assure,
That laughter in chaos, we must endure.
With a splat and a plop, we embrace the zest,
In shifting sands, humor's the best.

Lullabies from the Deep

A dolphin jumps, it spins with glee,
While I take a dip, and grab a seaweed tree.
My friend yells out, "What's that on your head?"
A floating starfish? I'll call it Fred.

The tide rolls in, with giggles and shouts,
As kids build castles, with moats and doubts.
But every wave teases their sand,
It's just a game, and oh, how it's grand!

Crabs on parade, they march along,
In perfect sync, it's their own song.
I try to step, join their silly beat,
Instead, I trip—oh, that's quite the feat!

Lullabies sung by the deep blue sea,
A chorus of creatures, wild and free.
As twilight falls, we dance on the foam,
Where laughter lingers, a seaweed home.

Currents of Time and Tide

The sun dawns bright, a brand new day,
With humor floating near, in every spray.
The beach is lively, all ages roam,
I step on a jelly, oh, what a home!

Skimming stones, trying to win,
But I just end up with a splash on my chin.
With friends beside, the fun won't cease,
As laughter erupts, we find our peace!

A toucan struts, a real show-off,
But one swift breeze makes him scoff.
With feathers ruffled, he takes a dive,
Oh, nature's humor keeps us alive!

Currents pull at our sandy toes,
In time and tide, the laughter grows.
So here's to the joy, the wild, and the free,
In this sunny paradise, we'll just be!

Riddles of the Ocean

Why did the crab take a nap?
It lost track of its own snap!
The fish giggled without fear,
While the seagull stole a pier.

The seaweed danced a silly jig,
Pretending it was quite a big pig!
Shells were laughing on the floor,
As crabs played chess with a door.

A dolphin wore a funny hat,
While starfish discussed their combat.
The octopus shared riddles bright,
The sea said, 'What a silly sight!'

And so the ocean chuckled loud,
As foam and bubbles formed a crowd.
With salty jokes from deep below,
The laughter echoed in the flow.

Solstice by the Shoreline

At noon the sun was feeling bold,
It challenged all the ice-cream sold!
With cones all melting in their hands,
The beachgoers formed silly bands.

A sandcastle wore a crown of shells,
While kids pretended to be wizards' spells.
The tide tickled toes with a splash,
As laughter soared like a lightning flash.

Seagulls squawked in their own way,
Stealing chips—'what a funny play!'
The sun said, 'Watch out for that tan!'
As beach balls bounced like a fan.

As twilight came with ice-cream stains,
The sun giggled, 'What are these gains?'
The horizon wore a smile wide,
And the ocean's secrets, none could hide.

Ripples in the Twilight

The moon went fishing with a grin,
And hooked a star—how rude! Oh, sin!
The tide tickled toes of the night,
As crabs performed their dance of fright.

A jellyfish wore polka dots,
As fish debated in funny knots.
The beachcomber lost his shoe,
While the tide laughed, 'Oh, how rude of you!'

The twilight whispered secrets bold,
Of clowns and mermaids, tales of old.
Seashells giggled with pride so grand,
While the sand told stories on command.

So when the sun starts its retreat,
Listen close—funny stories meet.
For in the dusk, laughter drifts,
And the ocean's joy, forever lifts.

Carved by Salt and Time

The rocks wore hats of seafoam green,
While crabs threw parties, what a scene!
Anemones danced to their own beat,
As turtles joined with tiny feet.

A barnacle claimed it was a king,
Declaring all shells had to sing.
The tide played tricks upon the sand,
As laughter soared across the land.

Time twisted stories, each ripple told,
Of fish in wigs and tales of gold.
The ocean chuckled in winds so swift,
As stars and shells began to shift.

And as the evening gently fell,
The sea shared secrets, spun a spell.
For carved by time, the fun lives on,
With salty jokes beneath the dawn.

Cradled by the Celestial Sea

In my floatie, round and bright,
I drift and giggle with delight.
A seagull steals my sandwich, too,
I yell, 'Hey bird, that's not for you!'

With every splash, I make a wave,
The lifeguard watches, quite brave.
My flip-flops fly, they're gone, oh dear!
Guess it's time for a souvenir!

Crashing Tides

The tide rolls in, like my cousin,
He trips and falls, it's quite the dozen.
He yells, 'Look out!' but nobody cares,
As he drags sand home in his hair.

Frisbees fly and kids all scream,
A beach ball bursts—what a bad dream!
With every crash, my drink spills wide,
But laughter can't be waved aside.

Whispering Currents

The water whispers secrets, true,
To crabs who dance in a daring queue.
I try to join, but lose my place,
And end up splashing foam on my face.

A sea turtle glides with grace and style,
While I flounder like a fish for a while.
'Is that a mermaid?' I giggle with glee,
It's just my buddy, wearing a seaweed tee.

Echoes of the Deep

Under the sun, my voice gets lost,
As I call to fish, at such a cost.
They flick their tails and swim away,
'Come back!' I shout, 'Let's laugh and play!'

The dolphins giggle, flip, and dive,
While I wriggle, trying to arrive.
Yet every flop, and every slip,
Is just another fun beach trip.

Embracing the Shimmering Surface

A fish wore a hat, so chic and so bright,
He danced on the sand under the moonlight.
Crabs snapped along, all stylish and spry,
While seagulls squawked tunes that made the fish sigh.

The clams had a ball, with shells shining proud,
Their conga line growing, attracting a crowd.
But someone got too close to the beach ball's cheer,
And went splashing in waves with a comical peer!

As laughter erupted, the tide rolled back in,
The fish wiggled happily, joined in the din.
They tossed back and forth, just for fun and a dare,
In a sea of delight, they launched from thin air!

So if you ever wander and hear a funny sound,
It's just the beach party where joy knows no bound.
Join the fish and the crabs, let your worries take flight,
In a world where the humor shines brilliantly bright.

Tales Written in Seafoam

Once a shark wrote stories in bubbles and foam,
Claiming the ocean was his grand home.
With tales of brave sailors and treasure galore,
He'd spin quite the yarn from the ocean floor.

The octopus giggled, with ink stains galore,
As he penned a fine novel by the old lighthouse shore.
But the fish were distracted, chasing their tails,
Turning plot twists into slimy fishy tales.

Even the starfish threw parties at night,
With disco lights shining, oh what a sight!
They danced to the rhythm of tides creeping near,
While the shark just rolled over, too full of his cheer.

And if you're out sailing, just look for the stars,
They might point to humor in the ocean's bizarre.
For each bubble is laughter, a tale full of glee,
In the realm of the sea, wild and free!

Moonlit Reflections on Water

The moon took a swim, all glimmer and glow,
While fish formed a chorus, putting on a show.
With lyrical bubbles and laughter so bright,
They serenaded the tide under the silver night.

A silly old turtle with shades on his face,
Said, 'Time for some fun, let's pick up the pace!'
So with a swift flip, he joined in the fun,
As dolphins leaped high, oh, the joy had begun!

But just when they thought they'd dance 'til the dawn,
A crab at the shore pouted, feeling withdrawn.
He shouted, 'I'm stuck in my old shell disguise!'
The fish swam around him, teasing his cries.

The moon just chuckled and turned up the beams,
As laughter erupted, spilling into their dreams.
For in the still water, reflections so clear,
Showed that laughter is magic when friends are near.

The Language of the Sea

In the depths of the ocean, you'd hear quite a sound,
As fish whispered jokes that danced all around.
'Tell me,' said the clam, 'do you have a new line?'
'How do you make a wave laugh? With a splash of good wine!'

The seaweed swayed, with curlies and twists,
Hearing all the tales of the ocean's funny risks.
An eel piped up, 'I'm slippery and slick,
I once slipped on a jelly; what a comical trick!'

A starfish flung out, 'I can't understand,
Why the fish got so nervous; why did he plan?'
As laughter erupted from those gathered near,
The octopus winked, 'I guess it's time for a beer!'

So remember, my friend, when you walk by the sea,
There's humor surrounding, just take it from me.
For the ocean's got tales that are wonderfully free,
And laughter is the language of the wild, boundless sea!

Shimmering Sands of Memory

Beneath the sun, the sand did glisten,
A crab scuttled by, oh what a mission!
It stopped and glanced, then made a dash,
As seagulls squawked, with a sudden crash.

Each grain a story, each laugh, a cheer,
I tried to dance, but tripped on my gear.
Rolled in the surf, oh what a sight!
My friends all laughed, what a pure delight!

The umbrella flew, I chased it fast,
Through giggles and shouts, it finally passed.
In the chaos, we found sheer joy,
Like kids with a new and shiny toy.

So here we lie, all sandy and bright,
Chasing our dreams into the night.
With memories made under the sun,
We laugh together, oh what fun!

Song of the Breaking Surf

The ocean sang with a gurgling tune,
A fish jumped high, beneath the moon.
I tried to catch it, with a swift swoop,
But landed instead in a splashing loop.

I donned my floaties, with style and flair,
Fighting the tide, I flew through the air.
My friend just chuckled, sipping her drink,
While I flailed wildly, not a second to think.

Seagulls overhead, they cawed with glee,
As I dog-paddled, not quite so free.
With algaes caught in a tangled mess,
I emerged, a sight hard to impress!

But through it all, we laughed till we cried,
As the sun dipped low, the shore our guide.
With each splash echoing a silly jest,
Our adventures here were simply the best!

Reflections on the Tuscan Mist

In a misty haze, the boats would sway,
I tried to row, but went astray.
Paddles tangled in laughter that day,
We sighed and giggled, while sunbeams play.

A squirrel stole snacks, it jumped on the deck,
Our sandwiches gone, oh what the heck!
With crumbs all around, we made a game,
An epic chase, oh what a name!

We sketched our dreams in the vapor's glow,
With silly faces, our spirits would flow.
Amidst the mist, we danced and twirled,
Two goofy pals, around the world!

And when the sun finally rose so bright,
Our hearts were full, oh what a sight!
With memories wet and smiles galore,
We laughed at the day, what fun we bore!

The Ocean's Gentle Caress

A friendly tide gave me a push,
Expected grace, instead a hush.
I flipped and tumbled beneath the foam,
Came up with seaweed, calling it home.

The lifeguard chuckled, what a grand show,
As I pretended I was a pro.
While others surfed, I did my dance,
In the splash zone, I took my chance!

The sun tickled my toes, a gentle tease,
Seashells beckoned, promising ease.
But I tripped and fell, lost to the sea,
Sending a message, just let me be!

With laughter echoing over the crest,
We gathered round for a post-dive fest.
Sandwiches shared, stories retold,
In the realm of joy, we felt so bold!

Celestial Currents

Blue blobs frolic in the tide,
As fish throw parties, oh what a ride!
Seashells gossip, laughing with glee,
While crabs dance the cha-cha, wild and free.

A dolphin declares, "I've lost my shoe!"
Mermaids giggle, saying, "That's not new!"
The sun then joins, a glowing balloon,
Together they sing a comical tune.

Starfish watching, they just can't decide,
Whether to wave or run away and hide!
With seaweed hats and a tide-pool throne,
This wacky beach dreams are never alone.

Underneath the Blue Canopy

Under the sky, where laughter resides,
Seagulls joke, their humor collides.
A crab claims its title, 'King of the Grit,'
With clumsy moves, it just can't quit.

Fish flip-flop, in a game of tag,
While turtles laugh, with shells all a-drag.
A clam shouts, "I'm a pearl in disguise!"
But no one believes, to their surprise.

Jellyfish do the tango in style,
With seaweed wigs that make us all smile.
Underneath this vast, blue canopy,
Life's a circus, and we're all so free!

Whispers of Old Sailors

Sailors recall tales spun with a twist,
Of mermaid barbecues none can resist.
With their fishy snacks and seaweed pies,
Each tale cracked up, with wide-open eyes.

One sailor claimed he'd caught a whale,
But it swam away, with a friendly tail!
Another inked a map, with a laugh and a wink,
To find where the neighbors had hidden their drinks.

Rum flows like tides through their stories told,
With punchlines poppin', both daring and bold.
Through bluster and puff, they sail on in glee,
These whispers of ages, just sailing the sea.

Parables of the Seashore

A crab once dreamed of flying high,
Claimed, "With a kite, I'd touch the sky!"
He tied some seaweed, took a jump and a leap,
But flopped on the sand, making quite a heap.

The starfish noted, "I'm lost in the scene,
Can someone tell me where my other arm's been?"
The gulls chuckled loud, as old shells applaud,
In parables spun with humor unflawed.

In this sandy space, where fun tales ignite,
The beach thrives on laughter, from morning to night.
So if you're feeling blue, just come take a stroll,
Follow the jests where the tides play the role.

Dunes and Dreams Beneath the Sky

Sandcastles crumbled, oh what a sight,
Seagulls giggled in pure delight.
Buckets and shovels in the game,
Who knew beach fun could be so lame?

Flipping a flop, the sunscreen flies,
Sandy hairdos and messy pies.
With every splash, saltwater sneezes,
Catching a wave ends with pure breezes.

Tanning upside down, we lose the tan,
Trying to swim, but drowning a fan.
Flip-flops thrown, into the sea's ruck,
Who brings a towel? We're just out of luck!

Laughter echoing, memories grand,
Making the best out of grains of sand.
With sunburnt noses and hearts so free,
It's the funniest place we could ever be!

Beyond the Breakers' Roar

Under the sun, we frolic and play,
Finding lost treasures that giggle away.
A crab in disguise, it pinches my toe,
I dance with the jellyfish, put on a show!

Surfboards wobble, we're on the move,
Balancing awkwardly, trying to groove.
An unexpected tumble, a sandy surprise,
I look like a mermaid with seaweed ties.

Floating on floats—such a silly bunch,
Eating ice cream for lunch with a crunch.
A pelican swoops, a crafty little thief,
Stealing our snacks, oh what a belief!

As the tide rises, we float like a cork,
Sharing dumb jokes while chomping a fork.
The ocean's our stage, laughs filling the air,
Who knew that freedom could also be rare?

A Journey to the Boundless Blue

Set sail on a float, with snacks at the ready,
Captain Clumsy here, steering unsteady.
A fish takes a nibble out of my leg,
Yelling 'I'm fine!' while I dance like a beg!

Splashes and giggles, the fun is afloat,
A wave's sneaky curl, oh no, my coat!
Riding the swells like a pirate's bold cheer,
But where's my treasure? Oh wait, it's beer!

Toasting with seafoam upon the high seas,
Swapping our stories, and feeling the breeze.
A dolphin pops up with quite the surprise,
Is it friendly or just a furry disguise?

Adventures are grand, with tales on the fly,
In the blue expanse, we laugh 'til we cry.
Returning ashore with memories amassed,
We'll treasure this journey until it goes past!

Footprints in the Grainy Gold

Stomping through grains like a toddler of fluff,
Every step leaves marks—are they ever enough?
A boogie in sand; the dance of a fool,
Who knew that the grain could become a cool pool?

Flip-flops gone rogue, they leap and they fly,
High-fiving the waves, they wave me goodbye.
Building a fortress, only to see,
The tide's cheeky grin as it laughs back at me.

Pies made of sand, what a perfect treat,
Just a pinch of salt and a crab for a feat.
We draw with our toes, silly shapes in the gold,
Making a mess, oh so carefree and bold.

Sunset approaches, painting the sky,
While footprints and giggles blend as they cry.
With laughter echoed where sand meets the fun,
These silly adventures, oh, they've just begun!

Secrets in the Foam

The sea's a joker, grinning wide,
It tickles toes and takes you for a ride.
Seagulls squawk with comic flair,
While little crabs perform their dare.

Shells sing secrets, whispers of cheer,
They laugh at clumsy tourists near.
Sand castles crumble with a splat,
As kids chase the tide, 'Hey, come back, cat!'

Starfish giggle, stuck in a pose,
While tanned folk rival beachy prose.
In the salty breeze, joy takes flight,
As flip-flops dance, the heart's delight.

Dance of the Aquatic Light

Bubbles bounce like giggly friends,
In a waltz where laughter never ends.
Fishy pranks in colors so bright,
Swirling around like kites in flight.

Splashing humor, a slippery tale,
Turtles twirl, without a scale.
Crabs are moonwalking, catching the beat,
As dolphins dive, oh what a treat!

Seashells spin, in the rhythm's embrace,
Each foamy jest, a new kind of grace.
Under the sun's warm, playful bite,
We join the dance, with all our might.

Rhythm of the Rising Blue

Gulls syncopate in wild formation,
While sunbathers nap, in sweet creation.
The tide rolls out for a laugh or two,
Making room for plans, and maybe a brew.

The ocean hums a cheeky tune,
As rafts float by, like balloons at noon.
Each splash, a joke, that ticks the clock,
As flip-flops slosh, it's all a shock.

Seagulls squabble, diving for fries,
Drawing laughs from wise old guys.
In this salty realm, all's a play,
With giggles and grins, come what may.

The Call of the Distant Horizon

From the shore, the view extends,
Where the horizon calls, and the fun never ends.
The ocean winks, 'Come play with me,'
As surfboards dance on glee's decree.

Sand flies high, like confetti in flight,
While beach balls launch into the light.
Kites soar high, a colorful spree,
While charming crabs just watch with glee.

The sun sets low in a regal bow,
The tide rushes in, we take a vow.
To laugh a bit louder, and splash about,
For the call of fun is what it's about.

Ebb and Flow of Silvery Light

A crab did dance on tiny toes,
With a shell like armor, striking pose.
The fish all laughed, a sight to see,
As seagulls cheered, "You're wild and free!"

Sunbathers laughed, their hats askew,
As a rogue wave chased their snack right through.
Sand castles swayed, then took a dip,
While children squealed and laughed, they zipped!

The breeze blew gently, tickling cheeks,
As flip-flops flung with squeals and shrieks.
The tide pulled back, a sly brigade,
As footprints vanished, what a parade!

Yet in the chaos, joy remains,
In salty air and sunny gains.
Each ebbing giggle, each flowing cheer,
A tale of fun from the coast so dear.

Beneath the Tidal Symphony

A sea turtle tried to sing a tune,
While fish debated 'round the moon.
The starfish sighed, "Don't make a scene,"
As octopi wore hats quite obscene!

Seagulls squawked, a raucous sound,
As they swooped low and stole the ground.
A picnic stolen, the snacks took flight,
While beachgoers laughed at their silly plight.

A whale popped up to crack a joke,
As jellyfish danced like silly folk.
The tide rolled in with giggles and grins,
Making every heart burst forth with spins.

So beneath this ocean's vast embrace,
There's always room for joy and grace.
Where laughter echoes, and fun aligns,
In nature's theater, all joys combine.

Glistening Secrets of the Surf

A hermit crab donned quite the flair,
In a borrowed shell, it had no care.
As waves rolled in, it strutted proud,
While clams clamped tight, beneath a cloud.

Mermaids whispered sly little schemes,
As dolphins spun in wild dreams.
They tossed a shell as a prize to claim,
And laughed as it fell, what a fun game!

Rubber ducks floated, without a frown,
As toddlers splashed and splashed all around.
A conch shell whispered, a hilarious tale,
Of seahorses racing, oh how they'd fail!

With every splash, the joy did grow,
Secrets kept in the surf's soft flow.
Each moment bright, with giggles to share,
In the playful heart of salty air.

The Meeting of Sky and Sea

The sun peeked down, a golden grin,
While clouds above looked quite akin.
A pelican swooped, wings a-flap,
Scaring tourists, oh what a trap!

Surfboards lined with eager folk,
In search of waves, excitement stoke.
But one went tumbling, a merry sight,
That left the crowd in pure delight!

A lighthouse stood, its beacon bright,
Winking at ships, all in its sight.
It chuckled low as seagulls dived,
To claim the fries, oh how they thrived!

So here we stand, where sea meets air,
In waves of laughter, joy to share.
As nature giggles, in its grand play,
We find humor, in every day.

Salt-Kissed Memories

Seagulls caw, they steal my fries,
Chasing crumbs like they're the prize.
Children squeal, they chase the tide,
While sandcastles begin to slide.

Laughter echoes, splashes fly,
As I squeak, a wet shoe sigh.
Someone's hat is whisked away,
Floating off, oh what a day!

A dog leaps high, its tongue a blur,
Chasing surf, oh, what a stir!
Sandy toes and salty hair,
Life's a joke, but we don't care.

As dusk descends, we pack our things,
With sunburnt cheeks and squeaky swings.
These memories stick, like gooey snack,
We'll come back each year, no looking back!

From Dusk to Aqua Dawn

Sipping drinks with cocktail flair,
A splash of juice flies through the air.
Someone's tumbling in the waves,
It seems like they forgot their knaves.

The sun dips low, a golden show,
As beach balls bounce and laughter flows.
Someone's shirt is lost, oh dear,
The tide's a thief, I hear a cheer!

Crabs scuttle fast, in pinch they play,
Is that a dance or a getaway?
We laugh at the antics, wildly fun,
Nature's jesting, and we've just begun!

Stars peek out, as night takes hold,
With tales of laughter and sand, retold.
We'll leave this place, but not our smiles,
For it's the fun that travels miles!

Nature's Chaotic Serenade

The wind's a joker, pulls my hat,
I chase it down, just like a cat.
Crashing sounds and squeals, oh great,
Dolphins giggle, it's a fishy fate!

A toddler slips, his ice cream flies,
He examines life with wide, bright eyes.
Sand in shoes and giggles soar,
Nothing but joy on this sandy floor.

The tide decides to hide my drink,
I laugh so hard, can't even think.
A jellyfish wiggles, what a sight,
A wobbly dance in moonlit night!

Shells are treasures, but oh, beware,
Some are home to creatures that stare.
A hermit crab hustles to escape,
Nature's chaotic, yet we can't wait!

The Breath of the Maritime

The sea breeze whispers tales untold,
A local crab struts, brave and bold.
Shells tumble, roll in sandy glee,
Look at me, look at me, says he!

Picnic baskets tip and sway,
Someone's sandwich, oh what a day!
As gulls swoop down to snatch a bite,
We laugh and scream, it's quite the sight!

Kids attempt to surf on foam,
While parents just enjoy their chrome.
With every splash, a joy takes flight,
This playful chaos feels so right.

As twilight kisses the gentle sea,
We pack our things, oh can't you see?
We'll cherish laughs and salty air,
In each heart's corner, humor's flair!

Soliloquy of the Sands

The grains conspire, in whispers they chat,
"Here comes the flip-flop, with its comical pat!"
They giggle at seagulls, so pompous and proud,
While crabs scuttle sideways, oh how they bow loud!

Sunny hats dance, sprouting like blooms,
As kites soar high, defying the glooms.
Sands slip through fingers, like jokes in the breeze,
And sunscreen debates, 'Who smells like cheese?'

A child with a bucket, making grand plans,
Building castles with moats, and guards: paper fans.
But a rogue little dog, with his squishy delight,
Turns that masterpiece into a snack for the night!

As laughter doth echo, the tide sneaks away,
Sands whisper secrets of joy and dismay.
Each footstep a promise, a tale yet to tell,
In the absurd theater where ocean waves dwell.

Old Bones and Ocean Secrets

A skeleton smiles, on the beach he lies,
With sunglasses and shorts, he's the king of the skies.
His old bony buddies all gather around,
For a game of beach volleyball, previously drowned!

A surfboard debates if it's time for a ride,
While flip-flops are plotting a counter-tide.
A seagull yells nonsense—it cracks up the crew,
And the crabs all unite for a spontaneous coup!

A treasure chest open, full of lost socks,
Says, "I found more than gold – just check out my stocks!"
They laugh and they cackle, throw seaweed like confetti,
As barnacles gossip about their new jetty.

Ah, the ocean's old secrets, a joke well-preserved,
In the laughter of sand, life's lessons curved.
And when the tide rolls back, just like our dreams,
We dance in the chaos, or so it all seems.

Rhythms of the Receding Tide

The water retreats, like a tough game of tag,
It winks at the sand, then gives it a brag.
"Can you catch me now? I'm running away!"
Sandy toes giggle, in playful display.

A jellyfish floats by, with style and grace,
His jelly-like jig is a memorable space.
While sand dollars gossip in hush-hush delight,
"Did you hear how shells talk? Their gossip's a fright!"

The gulls do a cha-cha, sashaying with flair,
As a kid in a bucket tosses water in air.
Flippers and fins join the whimsical crawl,
And crabs breakdance, posing all tall!

So with each ebb and flow of the giddy old sea,
Outrageous the rhythm, that laughter runs free.
Each splash tells a story, a giggle, a chime,
In the furious fun of the ocean's own rhyme.

Fragments of Forgotten Shores

Once a grand castle stood proud on the sand,
But the tide had some plans; it was not as it planned.
Now it's just fragments where memories play,
With shells interpreting what jesters would say.

A rubber duck floats, quite full of itself,
While lost flip-flops gather, neglected on shelf.
"Why do we wander?" one croaks with a grin,
"To find the right beach! Let's explore once again!"

In the chorus of laughter, fish learn to sway,
The crabs tell old stories of glory and fray.
With a laugher's parade under a bright sunny dome,
Even driftwood feels cozy, for here is its home.

So dance with the sand, let the ocean decide,
For every washed-up treasure, there's joy worldwide.
Embrace the fragments, let your giggles arise,
In the cryptic lore where humor never dies.

Whispers of the Tides

The sea has secrets, or so they say,
But all I hear is a fish's ballet.
A crab in a top hat, he winks and bows,
While seagulls perform their comedic routines with jowls.

Barnacles gossip on the old wooden pier,
While dolphins mock us with a splash and a cheer.
The octopus laughs, it's quite a hoot,
As he juggles seaweed like folks in a suit.

Now starfish argue who's best dressed for the show,
While sea cucumbers slide in a low-key flow.
Our flip-flops trip, our laughter we save,
For the tidal dance that the jellyfish gave.

But when the tide rolls in, oh what a tease,
The wet sand claims slippers, oh such a breeze!
We trip, we stumble, laughter won't cease,
At the whim of the tide, we're the clowns of the fleece.

Sand Between Our Toes

My feet are in a tussle, what a weird dance,
With grains of sand stealing my socks at a glance.
Seagulls squawk gossip as they strut in a line,
While I jump and skip, pretending it's fine.

The beach ball's plotting to fly with the sun,
While sunscreen rebels, oh what a run!
I slather it on like a cake on a plate,
And still manage to fry, isn't that fate?

I buried my friend, and now she's a mound,
As we laugh at her plight, what a sight we have found.
A sandcastle towers, oh what a grand dream,
Until the tide giggles and washes it clean.

But here in the sun, we giggle and joke,
As the beach becomes home to laughter and smoke.
With ice-cream drips down our shirts like a quest,
The mess on my face is a badge of my fest!

The Ocean's Gentle Embrace

The ocean waves tickle, oh what a prank,
They reach for my toes, then swiftly, they flank.
With floaties on heads, we look like a crew,
All while dodging crabs, how do they move?

The life guards whistle, just trying to show,
But the beach balls bounce, causing a real row.
In the splash zone here, it's a slippery feat,
As we challenge the surf in our flip-flop fleet.

A jellyfish dances, oh no, it's quite near,
But it floats like a balloon, never showing fear.
We squeal and we giggle, what madcap delight,
With sunscreen in eyes, we're a comical sight.

Yet underwater fish give us a smug glance,
As we flounder around, not quite in the trance.
The seaweed's a tickler, a green ribbon tease,
In this joyful escapade, we're always at ease!

Echoes of the Sea Breeze

A breeze flops my hat, it sails through the air,
As I chase after it, with laughter to spare.
The breeze plays tag with the seagull's wings,
While I yell at the tide, 'Hey, stop pulling these strings!'

A picnic forgotten, oh what a sight!
Sandwiches cringe as the gulls take flight.
Chips fly like confetti, oh what a clang,
As my lunch disappears with one zealous gang.

Now seashells whisper tales in the sand,
Of pirates that ventured, quite ill-prepared and bland.
With mermaids chortling, they splash in delight,
While sailors forever sleep, hugging their plight.

But here on the shore, with laughter my quest,
I dodge the umbrellas and take on the jest.
So raise a cold drink, let's toast to this whim,
For a day by the sea is never so grim!

Love Letters from the Ocean

Dear sandy toes, I wrote a note,
In seaweed ink, a love I wrote.
With every splash, my heart does race,
But seagoods swoop, oh, what a chase!

The shells conspire, they giggle and play,
As crabs join in, hip-hip-hooray!
Though fish can't read, their scales do shine,
I'm sending my love on fishy line!

So here's to our love, as salty as air,
With frothy giggles, we're quite the pair.
Oh, dolphin dance, let's make a scene,
In this ocean book, I'm your jelly bean!

So when waves crash, remember this beat,
For with every swell, we're still on our feet.
The tide rolls in with a goofy grin,
Dear ocean heart, let the fun begin!

Glistening Horizons at Dusk

The sun dips low, in its golden bed,
While seagulls argue, they're loud instead.
Two fish flip-flop, in a silly race,
While dolphins blow bubbles, making a face!

Shells collect stories, some giggly, some grand,
As crabs pull a prank, forming a band.
With blaring sea shanties, they sing off key,
Who knew the ocean's sounds, were so funny?

The stars appear, like sprinkles on pie,
While squids dance jigs, oh me, oh my!
The moon winks bright, with a cheeky spell,
As tides lead the way, to a shell-fish hotel!

At dusk, we laugh, like waves do peek,
In this sunset glow, there's joy to seek.
With every chuckle, our hearts collide,
In a sea of fun, we'll forever reside!

The Sigh of Distant Shores

Oh, listen close to the ocean's sigh,
As crabs giggle loudly, passing by.
A starfish dreams, on its lazy throne,
While otters play tag, never alone!

The sandcastle's wonky, a tower of dreams,
As kids splash about, in giggly themes.
A dog shakes off, spraying all around,
While seagulls squawk, calling it found!

The breezy whispers, full of delight,
Dancing with jellyfish, a charming sight.
They feast on the laughter, the sea's sweet hum,
With every ripple, more chuckles come!

So we'll gather here, beneath the sun's glow,
Where love blends with laughter, as soft currents flow.
When evening arrives, and the sky turns cool,
We'll snicker and splash, in this endless pool!

Captured by the Tide's Caress

The tide swept in, with a playful grin,
As I grabbed my float, ready to spin.
But a wave said, "No, that's not the way!"
In the splashy dance, I lost my sway!

The seashells chuckle, they roll on the sand,
While fishy folks frolic, making a band.
"Join us!" they chant, as they flit and swirl,
Who knew the tide could be such a girl!

With jellyfish jelly, we spread some cheer,
While sea otters spin, flipping without fear.
Crab legs wiggle, crabs dance round,
As laughter echoes, a seashell sound!

So let's capture this moment, a silly spree,
In the embrace of the tide, we're wild and free.
With giggles and splashes, we splash out loud,
In the ocean's heart, we'll forever be proud!

The Driftwood's Tale

Once a branch with dreams so grand,
It rolled and danced across the sand.
Claimed by a crab, it felt so cool,
Now it's the king of the! beachy pool.

It tells of fish that tell tall tales,
Of boats that sail with wind-filled sails.
But mostly it just sits and grins,
As seagulls plot their food-filled sins.

A starfish swears it knows the score,
While shells keep secrets of the shore.
Life's a comedy, or so it seems,
For driftwood rich with dreams and schemes.

So listen close, when the tide's just right,
You might hear laughter in the night.
For driftwood's wisdom weaves a song,
Of silly tides that flow along.

Knights of the Nautical Realm

In shiny shells, they gather 'round,
These knights of ocean, proudly crowned.
With swords of coral, they take a stand,
Protecting turf both beach and sand.

They joust with crabs, they dash and dive,
Each battle cry keeps them alive.
Gulls joke and jeer from high above,
While fish swim by in fits of love.

The seaweed flails, their flag unfurled,
As shells launch challenges to the world.
Yet at day's end, they sip on foam,
And plan their quests from their seaweed home.

With laughter ringing through the blue,
These knights delight in silly duels.
Beneath the sun, a jovial breath,
For nothing's grim in this watery depths.

Glimmers at Water's Edge

As the sun dips low, it starts to gleam,
The world mirrors a goofy dream.
Tiny fish in a swim parade,
With squishy sea cucumbers, unafraid.

Crabs do the cha-cha on the sand,
Renowned for their moves across the strand.
Seagulls squawk with comedic flair,
As they plot to steal snacks without a care.

The tide brings in both salt and fun,
Where laughter mingles, never done.
Mermaids giggle in the sea's embrace,
Creating mischief at a rapid pace.

At twilight's call, the stars align,
Casting giggles where the dolphins shine.
So join the party with joyous cheer,
For glimmers of laughter are always near.

A Lament for Lost Shores

Oh sandy spots where we would play,
Have washed away like dreams astray.
We sat and built our castles tall,
Now they've vanished, oh the gall!

The tide came in with a mighty roar,
And took my pail, oh what a bore!
I thought it safe right by my feet,
But the ocean laughs, and that's no treat.

Seagulls squawk, 'Oh dear, what a mess!'
As I stomp my foot in sandy distress.
I plead with fish with silly charms,
But they just flinch and flee from harms.

So here's to shores that danced and swayed,
We bid adieu, but not dismayed.
For every loss can yield some glee,
When sea and sky both jest with me.

Sonnet for the Sea Breeze

A seagull flew, stole my lunch today,
My sandwich now lost, a seagull's buffet.
The breeze it whispers, "Try a crab cake here!"
But crabs run fast, they have no sense of fear.

The ocean laughs, it tickles my toes,
As I trip over sand, nearly face-planting woes.
"Get up, you clown!" adds a child nearby,
I'll take that hit as I send out a sigh.

The tide rolls in, a watery tease,
It splashes my hat, what a perfect breeze!
"Surf's up," they shout, as I drown in delight,
Each splash is a giggle, a pure, silly sight.

Salty dogs bark, as they chase after fish,
I join in the chaos, like it's my own wish.
The sea, she's a prankster, and oh, what a show!
With splashes and laughter, just letting it flow.

Murmurs of the Underworld

Deep in the depths, where the odd fish roam,
Lurks a seaweed ghost, claiming this home.
"Boo!" it shouts loudly, giving fish the fright,
While the clams all cackle at this comical sight.

Octopus wears shades, flexing arms so bright,
"I'm cooler than you!" he says, trying to fight.
As bubbles float gently, making fish all burst,
"It's just too funny!" they chime, nearly cursed.

Crabs tap dance, moonwalking on the stones,
While jellyfish giggle in squeaky tones.
"Oh dear!" the eel hisses, "Just watch and see,
These gags get better, even for me!"

Anemones whisper of pranks from above,
As stars twinkle down like a hand from the glove.
In this underwater world, all doubts disappear,
With laughter in currents, and joy in the sphere.

Dunes and Dreams

In a desert of grains, I lost my flip-flop,
A rogue gust of wind just made that thing hop.
It flies like a bird, with no time for rest,
"Come back, my dear shoe!" I yell at my quest.

My towel's a sail, catching breeze with great flair,
While picnic ants scurry, they really don't care.
"Move over!" I shout, waving crumbs on my side,
They marched on my sandwich, I waved them a ride.

The sun's a joker, burns bright like a sign,
"Put on more lotion!" says my friend who's benign.
I slather it thick, then roll in the sand,
The look on my face? "Best plans slowly planned!"

The dunes tell stories of laughter and fun,
Where sunscreen is gold, and each joke's a home run.
So grab your beach toys, let's dance with the breeze,
For life is a laugh, it's full of such ease.

Fluid Melodies of the Coast

The tide hums softly, like a lullaby,
As flip-flops flounder, passing by the sky.
A crab croaks tunes, on its tiny guitar,
"Sandy Feet Blues!" echoes near and far.

The surfboards are giggling, catching some rays,
But flopping around, oh, what terrible ways!
"Surf's out!" shouts one, as they wipe out, they flop,
While seagulls all sing, at the beach they bop.

In a splash and a drift, oh, the fun we all make,
With sand castles crumbling, like a great birthday cake.
Whispers of laughter drift under the sun,
In this goofy rhythm, we all just have fun.

"More jelly!" cries someone, as we spot a new friend,
The sea is a joke, from beginning to end.
So give in to giggles, let your heart be so free,
For nothing's as merry as the coast that we see.

www.ingramcontent.com/pod-product-compliance
Lightning Source LLC
Chambersburg PA
CBHW072117070526
44585CB00016B/1484